FINISH

FINISH

AJ Bocchini

FINISH

Published by Wisdom House Books, Inc.
Chapel Hill, North Carolina 27514 USA
1.919.883.4669 | www.wisdomhousebooks.com

Wisdom House Books is committed to excellence in the publishing industry.

Book design copyright © 2019 by Wisdom House Books, Inc. All rights reserved.

Cover and Interior Design by Ted Ruybal

Published in the United States of America

Paperback ISBN: 978-0-578-61030-6
LCCN: 2019918601

BIO033000 | BIOGRAPHY & AUTOBIOGRAPHY / People with Disabilities
BIO016000 | BIOGRAPHY & AUTOBIOGRAPHY / Sports
SPO004000 | SPORTS & RECREATION / Basketball

First Edition

10 9 8 7 6 5 4 3 2 1

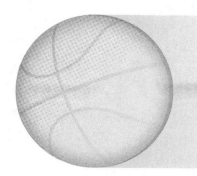

Table of Contents

The Magical Run

It was March 12, 2012, and we were in Salem, Virginia. The University of Wisconsin–Whitewater Warhawks were matched against Cabrini College of Pennsylvania for the NCAA Division III Men's Basketball Championship. Whitewater, led by head coach Pat Miller, trailed Cabrini College by 18 points with twelve minutes to go. Coach Miller decided to go to his bench and insert little-known freshman point guard Quardell Young. Q, as he was known by his teammates, was Coach Miller's last-ditch effort for giving the Warhawks a spark.

What happened next went so quickly that it remains a blur. From the twelve-minute mark on, the moments were magical. Q scored nine points in just over a minute, cutting Cabrini's lead in half. Game on! At that point, senior/Division III player of the year Chris Davis and our other playmakers took over. Battling back and forth for the next ten minutes, the Warhawks cut the lead to three with just over a minute left.

It was Davis's time to shine as he hit a big-time three to tie the game at 60. After this, the Warhawks got another stop. On the ensuing possession, we worked the ball around, finally getting it down to the post to senior Alex Edmonds. Edmonds took the ball hard to the hoop, laid it off the glass into the basket, and got fouled. After making the free throw, the Warhawks pulled ahead 63–60. With little time left, Cabrini had one last look, but the three-pointer bounced off the rim and the game was over. As we were celebrating on the floor that night, all I could think was that winning a national championship was a once-in-a-lifetime experience I would never forget.

The following season, we were fortunate enough to again make it to the tournament but were bounced in the second round in our attempt to repeat as champions. As we sat in the locker room at North Central College, I remember looking at my fellow juniors—Cody Odegard, Eric Bryson, and Alex Merg—and sophomores Steve Egan and Q, thinking to myself, *We will be back.*

Going into the following season as seniors, we had one mission: a national championship. That was our entire focus, at least on the court. For me, off the court was a little more difficult. Earlier that year, my uncle Jim had been diagnosed with ALS. To honor him that season, I remember writing his name on my shoes. I will always remember February 4, 2014. Stevens Point, our archrival and the number one ranked team in the country, was coming to town the next day. As I sat in my dorm room preparing to go to class, I got a call. My uncle had passed away. I sat there wondering what I should do. Do I call Mom and Dad to go home? Should I even be at the game tomorrow? After class, I went to head assistant coach Nick Bennett's office and met with him and Coach Miller. I told them about my uncle and asked what they thought I should do. After a great deal of thought and conversation, I did exactly what I know Uncle Jim would have wanted me to do, which was manage the team to victory. I decided I was all in.

Waking the next day, I felt like something special was about to happen. Battling from behind the entire game, we tied in the last few seconds to push the game to overtime. We battled back in overtime, down 4 with under a minute left. In the end, we pulled out the win. Even with this win, we finished second in the conference that season, but this game gave us the confidence that we could make another deep run in the Division III Championship. Finishing second didn't allow us any breaks as far as seeding or home court advantage, but this was exactly what we needed—to be the underdog and have to grind out wins. Fast forward four wins later, and the group of now seniors and juniors was back in Salem for its second Final Four in three years.

After a tough battle defeating Illinois Wesleyan in the national semifinal, we were facing Williams College in the national championship game. Williams was led by freshman sensation Duncan Robinson. After the season, Robinson transferred to the University of Michigan on a full scholarship with the Wolverines. This was a game for the ages, going back and forth the entire time, seeing numerous lead changes. The final seconds were a swing of emotions. Warhawks junior Steve Egan got a steal to give us the ball back, but we weren't able to score on the possession. With Williams down by one, it was Duncan Robinson's time. Robinson took the ball off the dribble and pulled up what looked like a game-winning jumper. The ball rolled off the rim, but teammate Michael Majer tipped it in with 4.8 seconds left, putting Williams up by one. At that time, most coaches would have called timeout to draw up a play, but not Coach Miller. After the ball went through the hoop, Egan—without hesitation—inbounded a quick pass to Q.

Going coast to coast in a matter of 3.9 seconds, Q drove to the basket, banking it off the glass for the game winner. For the second time in three years, we had made history. Team members Q, Cody, Eric, Steve, and Alex Merg, along with Coach Miller and our trainer Steve, became two-time national champions. The final two-time national champion on that team was me, AJ Bocchini. I was the manager of those teams, and I am the one writing this story.

The national championships are far from the beginning of my story, and I'd like to share my journey here with you. I hope you'll enjoy it and perhaps find yourself a little more motivated to drive for success.

2 FINISH
How Did It Come About?

I was fortunate enough to be surrounded by a great group of college teammates. We grew up together. Many of us were in the same class or on the same level of our careers. As we grew as a team, I felt more comfortable growing into a leadership role. In that leadership role, which my teammates allowed me to have—this is where FINISH came into play.

The day before our second national championship game in 2014, we were warming up, getting ready for the big game. It was going to be our last shootaround of the year. As practice was ending, Coach Miller pulled us into the huddle for some final words. Before he got going, he looked at me and said, "AJ, what's your final message to the team?"

I paused and looked up at the ceiling before I replied, "We have come so far and overcome so much. We've faced a lot of adversity this year, and now it's time to FINISH the deal."

The next day, we won our second NCAA Division III National Championship out of the past three tries.

So how did FINISH live on? Later that spring, the team came together for our annual banquet. Coach Miller kicked off the ceremony by congratulating and complimenting all of us for coming together as a team. After this, he started speaking about a special inscription inside the championship rings. He reminded us of that day before the National Championship game, of what I had said to the team at that final huddle before the game. He told the audience that my words and telling the team to FINISH will always be remembered, especially now that the word FINISH is inscribed in the inside of each team member's NCAA Championship ring.

After that day, I thought long and hard about what FINISH really meant to me and how I could transform it into something I could live by. Hopefully, as you read on, you will understand what drove me—and just maybe it will drive you to FINISH every day.

The Starting Five

When people talk about a starting five, they are most likely referring to the starters on the basketball court. I always remember the University of Michigan's team, which was referred to as the Fab Five during the time I was growing up.

When I use the term starting five or Fab Five, I think of my family. I see each of them playing a position in my life, starting with my parents, Lisa and Doug, the two most influential people I know. My mother played defense, as no one could protect her family better than she. My dad was our assist man. He brought us up in sports with the belief that no one was individually bigger than any other person; all the members of his teams were on an equal playing field. What I love most about my parents is how, on the one hand, they are two of the most supportive and loving people you will find, and on the other hand, they're not afraid to push us to be successful.

Now for my two brothers. Douglas worked the paint. He was the oldest, and he controlled the game by setting the tone for us brothers. Being the oldest, he was the first to fall in love with sports. In high school, he played soccer and basketball, and he ran track. I was fortunate to be close enough in age that I would later be a part of the same high school basketball team with him for three years. As I followed in my brother's footsteps, my younger brother followed in mine. He was the scorer. He took the best of both of us and made his own mark. Dom, like me, followed a successful high school career by running track at UW La Crosse. He, again like me, has two national championships of his own, but his are on the track.

Being the middle of three boys was a big responsibility. My job was to be Mr. Consistent. Not only did I follow the example set by Douglas, but it was also my job to set an example for Dominic. The best part about my family is that I was AJ; there were no wheelchairs or limitations or disabilities in their eyes. To this day, most of Douglas's friends in Colorado, where he moved a few years ago, don't know I am in a wheelchair. I am just his younger brother.

Every starting five needs a great sixth man. Our team wouldn't be complete without Ace, our golden retriever. Like most sixth men, he outhustled everyone on the court. Ace was best known for going outside and patrolling the entire neighborhood in the middle of the night. As you can probably guess, like most families, we were pretty tight, especially with our passions and common interests.

While my brothers and dad were influential in terms of my love of sports and the passion for what I now hope will be my long-term career, there was one family member who helped me through the struggles of having cerebral palsy (CP) growing up. That influential person was my mom. From the day I was born, Mom served and continues to serve as not only my mom but also as my biggest fan, supporter, and advocate. To understand what it's like to have CP in my family, you need to understand that my mom's role was to make me the best person possible. Twice a week, for as long as I can remember, my mom has taken me to physical therapy. Looking back, I didn't like it because I wanted to be with all my friends at school—running around, hanging out, and playing sports. Sometimes I would miss high school practices because I had therapy. This was not something I chose to do, but my mom knew what was best for me. Being older now, I understand the value in physical therapy, and I understand the sacrifices my mom made to get me there every week. The miles she put in during all those years of getting me to therapy, games, and doctor appointments in Milwaukee were amazing. Wherever I needed to be, whenever I needed to be there, Mom always took care of me. My brothers made sacrifices for me over the years as well. The time they missed with mom, I never truly understood or appreciated until I was older. I can't thank them enough. Finally, somehow my dad continued to be there for all of us whenever we needed him the most. He was our coach, our leader, and the breadwinner.

So, when I think about my starting five, plus our sixth man Ace, I think about how they allowed me to be myself with no hesitation. Being "just AJ" made growing up easy. I believe the only time I was truly recognized as being in a wheelchair was when I was called out for my bad driving. But that is for another chapter.

ACE
Family and Best Friend

When we hear people talk about best friends, they often are referring to a brother, sister, classmate, or relative. I think if you ask the three Bocchini boys who their best friend was growing up, we would say he had four legs and a golden coat. This would be no other than our first dog, Ace. To understand the relationship between Ace and our family, we have to go back to when I was eight years old.

It was the fall of 1999, and my parents started looking for a service dog to help me with daily tasks around the house. As I loved to play catch, we were hoping we could find a dog who could catch, retrieve a tennis ball, and bark when I needed help.

Mom and dad started looking for a dog by doing some research and making phone calls. Our travels took us to a minimum-security prison outside of Green Bay, which specialized in training service dogs. Our visit was really exciting. After touring the facility, we were able to meet a couple of dogs who could do amazing things. Our favorite was a beautiful yellow lab who could perform several tasks, from picking up remotes when the trainer pointed a laser, to opening a refrigerator and bringing a soda to the trainer. Of course, we were hoping to take that dog home. Problem was, he was their show dog. Next, we got to meet several other dogs: black labs, yellow labs, and golden retrievers. Finally, a beautiful golden retriever named Ace walked into the room. It was love at first sight.

We went right to the head trainer and told him about our choice. Now came the tough part. The trainer advised us that Ace needed to stay at the facility for the next several months to be trained and get ready to work with me. Although this was difficult, we knew it was the right thing to do.

As part of the training, we would go visit at least once a month, spending a few hours with him so he would get to know us. We were also able to bring him home periodically for the weekend so he could get comfortable with me and our house. Seeing Ace was always a lot of fun.

Finally, after several months, it was graduation day for Ace and several of his other friends. The local newspaper and TV station were coming to do a story about this exciting day. It was time for Ace to come home with us. The next thing that happened is not what we expected. When we came through the door, the first person Ace ran to was my older brother, Douglas. That ended up being the picture in the newspaper. This is when we realized Ace wasn't necessarily my service dog, as had been intended.

What we first thought might just be a mistake on Ace's part turned out quickly to be reality. As much as I tried to play fetch, Ace didn't like tennis balls. As much as we tried to get him to bark when I needed help, he didn't bark. As much as I tried to do training with Ace, it soon became clear that this dog was different. No tennis balls, no barking, no training. Ace had no interest in becoming a service dog. Instead, he just wanted to be the best family dog we could have ever imagined. His personality fit in with the rest of the family.

Periodically, the head trainer called us to see how Ace was doing. We were always afraid if we told him the truth, they might take him away. Instead we would just say, "He's fitting right in with the family."

For the next ten years, we all grew up with Ace by our side. He was our best friend. In addition, Ace did something I believe will be true for the rest of my life. He gave us the okay to grow up.

Fast forward to Labor Day weekend, 2010. Douglas was heading back to University of Stevens Point for his sophomore year, and I had moved to University of Wisconsin–Whitewater to begin my freshman year. On that Tuesday evening, Dominic was at football practice with Dad, leaving Mom at home with Ace. Mom was in the bedroom putting away clothes when she heard a howl and a bark, as if Ace were chasing a rabbit. When she came out to see what was going on, she saw him lying in front of the fireplace. It was then she realized Ace was not breathing. He had passed away.

Our neighbor, Dr. Bohn, was Ace's vet. Mom called him immediately, and he came right over to our house. He had told Mom only a month earlier at his annual checkup that Ace was healthy. Now Dr. Bohn told Mom, "With all that's going on, I truly believe that Ace died from a broken heart."

As time passed, rather than take a dim view of what happened, I looked at this as Ace telling us it was okay to grow up. It was as if he were saying, "I've done all I can for you guys; now go chase your dreams. I'll be looking down and finally chasing tennis balls." Ace was a huge part of our lives.

If it weren't for him, there's no telling how our lives would have been different. For most people, a dog is part of the family and a valuable member of their team. There's no doubt Ace was that to us . . . but he was something more. He was a best friend to a kid who was once 3 lbs. 14 oz. He was definitely the sixth man we could all count on.

Later, you'll read about my lake experience and several other driving adventures I have had. During all these times, Ace was there to make me laugh.

Ace may have not chased balls, played catch, or barked when I needed help, but he wasn't an ordinary dog. He was quite simply, Ace, our best friend.

5

You Can Call Me AJ

As most people know, the first thing you do when meeting somebody new is start the conversation by introducing yourself by your first name. Many times, I wonder how people received their first name. Were they named after Grandma or Grandpa, Mom or Dad, a favorite aunt or uncle, a movie star, an athlete, or a friend? What you'll find out is that almost everyone has a story to tell regarding how they got their names.

To understand the beginning of my story and my journey through life, you need to know the story behind my name. It all started on December 19, 1991. I was born two months prematurely, at 3 lbs. 14 oz. Originally, I was supposed to have been born in mid-February, so I became Mom's Christmas gift rather than her Valentine's day present. My mom tells me that up until a week before I was born, it seemed like a normal pregnancy with no issues or complications.

Because I came early and caught my parents off guard, they still weren't sure what name they were going to give me. The decision became easy as my parents watched me hooked up with tubes, wires, and oxygen, fighting to make it through these early days. It was at that time that they named me Anthony Joseph after my two grandfathers, Anthony Bocchini and Joseph Miller. These were two successful men who grew up with a great deal of adversity in their lives. They worked their tails off for their families, and both had the similar common characteristic of being stubborn as hell and never giving up. I'm convinced these characteristics were passed on to me, even in my early days at the hospital.

So then, how did my name go from Anthony Joseph to AJ? Being born eight weeks early, I had to spend almost five extra weeks at the hospital. One morning, when my parents returned to the hospital after a night at home, they were looking for me in the NICU, trying to find "Anthony" on the crib. When they finally found me, they noticed that someone had changed my name to AJ. In talking to the nurses, my mom and dad inquired as to why they had changed my nameplate. One nurse stated, "He's too small for such a long name, so we shortened it for him." From that day forward, the name AJ stuck. Twenty-six years later, many of my friends still don't know that my real name is Anthony.

Even though AJ stuck, my actual name isn't diminished. Just like my grandfathers, I had a great deal of adversity at an early age. But, also like my grandfathers, I have the fight and stubbornness to be successful. Little did I know that the never-give-up attitude I had in the hospital would set the tone for the rest of my life—and my journey was just beginning.

6

Family Name Over Money and Fame

Growing up as a kid in Kohler, Wisconsin, I had big dreams. I would sit down and watch a sporting event featuring Brett Favre and the Packers or Michael Jordan and the Bulls and think, *Someday I will be there.* As I grew up, I quickly began to realize that playing professional sports would not be an option due to my physical limitations. Like many boys my age, I dreamed of money and fame earned by playing a game. Now, as a young man out of college, my dream is different. I realize that I represent my family's name. My name is AJ Bocchini. I was not raised a Favre or a Jordan. I don't play and coach sports for money or fame. I do what I love to represent my family's name.

Whatever your passion is, don't strive to excel in hopes of chasing someone else and being better than they are. Instead, perfect your passion to make a name for your family and leave a legacy they can be proud of. We all go through ups and downs. We all have challenges. During my ups, downs, and challenges, I know one thing has never changed: Bocchini is my family's name, and that's who I represent every single day.

Throughout the course of life, your challenges, friendships, and obstacles may change. We may work for different teams, companies, or organizations. As you're sitting down to read this, I hope you take this thought away with you: the one thing that will never change is your family's name. Represent it to the best of your ability, and realize that you're setting an example for those who will one day have your name as well. Life and goals should never be about money and fame. They should always be about the family name.

The Doctor's Appointment That Defined Me

In life, we all have those key moments that can be either good or bad—moments that help shape us into the people we are today. When I talk to people and share my story, they often ask me, "What moments stick out in your mind that helped make you who you are now?"

I definitely think about growing up in Kohler and playing sports with my brothers and friends, being the manager for two national championships, and getting my master's degree. For all those great moments, however, there is one key moment that sticks out in my mind.

In 2000, when I was nine, my parents took me to Minnesota for a weekend to go through some tests to find out more about my CP. Mom and Dad said that at the end of the weekend we would meet with a doctor to discuss the test results and what could be next. After two days of testing and the weekend winding down, we went in to meet with the doctor. What he was about to tell me would change my life forever. I can remember it distinctly. He looked at me and then at my parents and said, "Your son will never be able to walk." I saw the concern and disappointment on my parents' faces. I don't think any of us remembers anything else the doctor said after that statement. We left his office, totally quiet, not quite knowing what to say. I quickly found that the doctor's statement that day created a chip on my shoulder. That day gave me motivation; it was one of the most defining moments of my life.

The doctor told me that I couldn't do something . . . and I proved him wrong. Later that year, after a great deal of hard work, I was able to walk with the use of a walker. I actually walked down the aisle for my First Communion, although afterward I quickly started using a power wheelchair, as it is more efficient. For that one day, I know I proved that doctor wrong, if only for a short time. Ever since then, when somebody tells me I can't do something, I don't get angry. I remember that day and use it as motivation. By never forgetting, I can go back to that moment and chalk it up as another doubter proven wrong.

Most people will tell you to block out the doubters. I like

to take a different approach. Hear them, but don't listen to them. Spend time with those who believe in you, and chase your successes with them. Use the doubters as motivation, and achieve your goals despite those who think you can't.

A lot of people can start the journey to their goals when others tell them they can do something. Very few people can finish their goals in the face of those who tell them they can't. Remember to lean on those who have believed in you from the start, because they will be the ones who will help you get to your goals and ultimately to the FINISH.

Don't Let Your Challenges Dictate What You Do

I know some of you will look at the title of this chapter and say, "What the heck is he talking about?" Allow me to explain. As I mentioned, I was born two months prematurely with CP, which is caused by damage to the motor cortex of the brain—the part of the brain that affects muscle control and coordination. This, no doubt, placed a challenge on me early on in life. From a young age, I was taught one simple thing by a great group of people also known as my family. They said, "AJ, you have two choices: you can either allow yourself to turn your challenge into a strength and use it as a positive, or your challenge can become a weakness that you use to fall back on when things go bad." Let's just say I chose the first one.

It was with the help of many that I took the CP challenge and made it into a strength. My parents and my brothers viewed me as if I didn't have CP. They didn't see a challenge in my life. I was AJ. As far as the wheelchair, it was just my way of getting around, nothing more. It was just another strength in my life. I never allowed myself to have a weakness. There were no limitations to what I could do. We just found a way. This carried over to the classroom and my social life with my friends. They never saw the wheelchair. I remember playing kick ball at lunch hour with our principal, Mr. Jeff Dickert, pitching. I had a designated kicker and I ran the bases. My friends just saw a way for me to play. The only challenge I seemed to bump up against regularly was my driving skills, which my friends and family pointed out to me regularly, with a smile on their faces.

My parents also expected me to perform well in the class-room. I had some of the best aides. They helped me be an outgoing person and succeed, never seeing the chair as anything more than a way to get from point A to point B. It was with their help and support that I am where I am today. I also found that when I pushed and challenged myself, I often inspired those around me. Over time, I realized I could use my challenge as a platform to show what is possible in a power chair.

So, you might ask, "What is your point?" Everyone has chal-lenges. Some are more visible than others. When presented with those challenges, we have two options. Use them as a positive influence on other people or use them as a way to negatively affect other people around you. If we choose the earlier option, we can make a greater impact on people on an even larger scale.

I have learned to make obsolete the "dis" in the word dis-ability and focus on the word ability . . . the ability we have to make a positive impact on our families, friends, and people we don't even know. The ability, regardless of what you're going through—whether a physical, mental, or per-sonal challenge—to turn it into a strength. The ability to understand that we may not fully be aware of why we were given our circumstances, but there's always a reason, and we need to make the best of it.

Now, go out and compete in this game of life. Run your own race, and always remember to FINISH what you started.

Wheeling the Ground Running

A new start, a new job, or even a new car can be seen as a chance to hit the ground running. For me, the opportunity to be mobile without help came with new transportation. Consequently, the name of this chapter is "Wheeling the Ground Running."

Let me take you back to December, 1996. With the way my life is now, it's only appropriate that my first wheelchair experience and the game I love crossed paths to create one of my earliest memories of being in a chair.

My dad was the Kohler High School girls' junior varsity basketball coach. On Saturday mornings, he would take my older brother Douglas and me to practice so we could hang out and watch the team. You see, many of those girls were our babysitters. Katie, Corey, Pam, or Emily were frequently at our house, watching the Bocchini boys.

On this particular Saturday morning, shortly after practice

started, Douglas, who was six at the time, checked with my dad to see if it was okay for him to push me around in the gym in my new wheelchair. My dad saw this as no big deal. Boy, was he wrong. Douglas asked me if I wanted to go for a spin around the gym. Being young and wanting to be entertained, I naturally agreed. It was my older brother's idea after all. It had to be a good one! As most of us have learned, all plans sound good until something goes wrong.

This is exactly what happened: What started as a quick spin around the gym turned into my brother's pushing me at top speed. The straight away was fine. However, once we hit the turn, one of my wheels left the ground, I tipped, and the chair and I went flying. I remember the THUD sound as my body and head hit the floor. My glasses flew off, and my head was bleeding like crazy. Needless to say, practice was stopped. Dad, in addition to all the players/babysitters, went into action. The next thing I remember, I had a towel wrapped around my head and my mom was holding me tight in the van as our family friend Beth Pierce drove me to the hospital to get stitches. The highlight of a new chair turned into a lowlight for me. Practice ended early, though, and I am still not sure if it was a lowlight for the girls.

Though the chair survived the crash, I have the scar to remind of what would be the first of several exciting wheelchair rides.

10 Wheeling the Ground Running (The Sequel)

As I stated in the previous chapter, I thought crashing my manual wheelchair was a one-of-a-kind experience. I didn't think anything could top that. Who knew my first time in my power wheelchair would compete for such a memory?

For someone to earn their driver's license, they first need their temporary license. That may also be a good idea when someone drives a power wheelchair for the first time.

I remember the day like it was yesterday. I was in second grade and had to be pushed around to get wherever I needed to go. I was finally getting a power wheelchair, allowing me to get from point A to point B on my own. I was so excited as they delivered it to my school. Mrs. Dexheimer (Mrs. D., my long-time aide) and my mom were there watching as the wheelchair technician put the final touches on it. Finally, I was placed in the chair. The technician looked at me and without further instructions said, "Okay, drive!!" I remember his toolbox a few feet in front of me and a very large milk cooler to my right. Without any hesitation, I took off, creating one of the craziest memories I've ever had. I went full speed, over the technician's toolbox, and then proceeded to hit the giant milk cooler, which weighed several hundred pounds, moving it twenty feet and ripping a socket right out of the wall. When I finally stopped, there was Mrs. D. and Mom, mouths wide open, not knowing what to say. The wheelchair tech just looked at me and said, "Well, I think we need to turn down the torque." That was an understatement and a little too late. Moving forward, people often question my ability to drive straight. Looking back, I laugh and remember thinking, *I am going to need a lot more practice.*

In life, there will always be new skills to learn, obstacles to face, and challenges to overcome. When they come, you just have to keep moving forward, and eventually things will straighten out. Don't give up on it; just keep pushing. If you do that, you will get to a level that will make the skill second nature to you. All it takes is a little patience, persistence, and practice. And maybe a tool kit to run over and a milk cooler to move.

11 LESSON ONE IN SCIENCE: Water and Electricity Don't Mix

When I was young, my wheelchair technician told me, "Don't get your chair wet; if you do, you will be without." Like most ten-year-olds, I was pretty active. I used my chair to keep up with my friends, my brothers, and my dog Ace. That summer was no different—or so I thought.

One night, we decided as a family to go on an early summer evening walk with Ace. We decided to walk around the lakes of Woodlake in the village of Kohler where we lived. What started out as a normal walk ended as anything but. I ran ahead to follow Ace. As normal, I was moving along at top speed. All of a sudden, Ace stopped, dropped, and began rolling around in the grass. As I came to a quick stop, I started laughing as Ace continued to roll. The next thing I knew, I bumped my joystick, turning my chair toward the lake, and away I went—down the bank and into the water.

Thankfully, Douglas was not far behind. He jumped in the lake, turned my chair upright, and got me out of the chair.

My parents and Dominic came running to help me out. Being so young, my first reaction was being totally scared about being stuck in the chair, underwater. What didn't register in my mind were the ramifications of what had just happened to the chair. My mom and I sat on the side of the lake while Douglas, Dominic, and Dad pulled the chair out of the lake and got it back on dry land. We automatically tried starting it up, but it made a buzzing noise and then nothing. It was fried.

I remember sitting in the van, shivering, a traumatized ten-year-old kid. The thought of being strapped in the wheelchair under water was so scary. To this day, I swear I saw a fish swim by.

The same wheelchair tech who reminded me to stay away from water came out within a couple days to check it out and give me the news. "Power wheelchairs and water do not mix. Your chair is fried, and you're going to be without it for three months." I was devastated. My mobility was taken away from me for the entire summer. Luckily for me, my brothers again stepped up and made sure I was still a part of everything. Although being powerless was very difficult, they made it okay.

I learned a lot of lessons during this experience. First, keep your power chair away from large bodies of water. Second, always take care of your things, especially those that directly impact your success. Third, family is everything. The summer without my chair would have been a lot more difficult had I not had my brothers, my parents, and of course, Ace. They allowed me to continue to move forward.

Without my usual mobility and independence, that summer was hard, but I made the best of it and used the tools I did have to make up for the tools I did not have at my disposal. Sometimes, you have to find the way to make yourself successful despite your obstacles.

12

Whitewater, the Ride, and the Curb I Will Never Forget

When I talk about the University of Wisconsin–Whitewater, I have so many great memories, such as the friends I made, receiving my bachelor's and master's degrees, and winning two national championships, just to name a few. However, it was several years before I actually started attending UWW that I had my first—and most memorable—experience. The same summer I fried my wheelchair at Woodlake, there was a ride at UWW I will never forget.

My passion for sports is endless. However, being in a chair at a young age, I didn't know exactly how to get involved. My parents were looking for a way for me to get different experiences. They discovered a wheelchair sports camp at Whitewater. Going away to camp at age eight was going to be exciting, but no doubt I was a little scared.

For the most part, I loved camp . . . during the day, that is. At night, I would have a tendency to get homesick because I was so young. Thankfully, Tracy Chenowyth, the camp director, and the rest of the staff were always around to keep me company.

It wasn't until the third time I went to camp that I was really excited about it. I was finally comfortable enough that I wasn't going to get homesick. This year, I was really going to be on my own because my parents were heading to San Francisco for a few days. My dad had some work, and Mom was going to join him for a couple of extra days of relaxing.

As I said earlier, for the Bocchini's, a fried wheelchair wasn't going to slow me down. Mom jumped on the phone with the UWW camp, advising them what had happened. Because I had been there before, Tracy told Mom, "Just send him down in his manual chair. We will take care of him."

As camp began, I was fired up to make new friends and have more awesome experiences. What happened that first night put the entire week in a tailspin. We were getting ready to go to a Brewers game that evening. It was going to be great. Shortly after my mom dropped me off, a group of us outside the dining hall decided to play frisbee golf. Now, if you can picture this, I am in my manual chair, with (as I found out later) only one brake on as a safety precaution. When play began, I felt my chair start to roll. It picked up speed. Being naïve, I thought *This is cool! I'll go over the curb and land some sweet trick.*

As you can imagine, that isn't exactly what happened. Instead, I hit the curb and went face down into the concrete. The results were catastrophic to my camp experience and Mom and Dad's trip. I ended up with a broken jaw. Fortunately, Mom had not left for her trip, so my camp experience lasted all of ten hours before she picked me up in the middle of the night. Dad, who was already in San Francisco, took the red eye home. The next day, I was in the emergency room with my mouth wired shut. Those wires were supposed to stay on for eight weeks. Those who know me can attest to my inability to stop talking. I was back in the clinic two weeks later, on the 4th of July, to have them removed. I guess when your mouth is wired shut, you should not talk a lot. Not my strong point.

If you would have told me after that experience that I would end up at UW–Whitewater for college, I would've laughed. What I can I say is that every time I went to the dining hall over the course of my six years of undergraduate and graduate school, I looked down at that curb and said, "Remember me? You thought you could stop me from coming here, but I'm back." I will never forget that curb because it was my first experience of adversity at the place I would later call my second home.

13 Leveling the Playing Field

Ask any person with a disability and, if they're honest, they'll tell you it's important to have an activity that helps level the playing field. By this, I mean an activity which diminishes the disability and allows them to focus on their passion for what they love to do.

Growing up, I was able to level the playing field through sports. When I was on a court or on the field, the challenge was the opponent, not the CP. Anyone who has been around me will tell you I'm one of the most competitive people you'll ever meet. I hated losing so much that I couldn't stand it, and most people couldn't stand being around me when it happened. I'm not exactly sure what made me this way. Was it that I viewed sports as an outlet to help me overcome my CP? Maybe it was the household I grew up in, or more than likely it was because I wanted nothing to hold me back, promising myself I would always give maximum effort. I'm not sure which one it was. What I did know for sure was that when I was part of a sports team, there was no CP. There was only one thing to do: give my best effort for my teammates and those who believe in me.

That's exactly what I did. I played everything growing up: football for coaches Dan Buhr and Duane (Butch) DuMez, soccer and track for my mom, and basketball for my dad. As with any competitive career, there were many highs and lows.

It was the fall of my fifth-grade year, and I was playing both soccer and football with the help of Mom and Dad. As I wasn't able to play in my chair, my parents carried me under my arms, working to get up and down the field. For soccer, my mom would swing me like a foosball player, using my legs to kick the ball on defense. This season, I had grown a little bigger, making it harder for my parents to carry me around on both fields. Like any young athlete, there comes a point in your career where they may have to choose between sports and what they want to play growing up. For me, that decision was made that day in Oostburg on the soccer field. It was at this time that my lowest and possibly most embarrassing moment in sports came. My mom swung me like a foosball player so I could kick the ball. Instead of getting the ball, I connected with the face of a player from the Oostburg team. The game stopped. No one could comprehend what had happened. I felt terrible, but I know Mom felt even worse. From that point forward, my soccer career was over, and I transitioned strictly to football and track. For as much fun as I had on the soccer field, I knew growing up that it was to be short-lived.

With football and track, I could be a success on my own with the use of my power wheelchair. I was fortunate to have many people who didn't see the chair. One of those people was Coach DuMez. Coach was the first person who found a way for me to contribute on the football team in middle school. He placed me as the punt returner, allowing me to make an impact on the game on special teams. Coach DuMez put me in a position to make me successful regardless of how it was done. The best memory I have of middle school football was when we played at Elkhart Lake. I played my usual position: punt returner. At one point, I was able to return the ball all the way to the one-yard line. I was headed off to the sidelines when all of a sudden coach sent me back out, and told me to run it up the gut. I scored our first touchdown of the year.

My success in football carried over to middle school track. This was a lot of fun, especially with Mom, Coach Eric Eckert, and Coach Frantz Felix being the coaches. Every day was a lot of work, but it was always entertaining. Coach DuMez was the head high school track coach, and he was instrumental in allowing me to run in the middle school meets, as some schools were concerned that my power wheelchair would tear up their rubberized track.

The highlight of middle school track was taking third in the mile. I had an eight-minute mile, securing a point for my team. I loved track. It was all about speed, and there was no one you were competing against except yourself. I loved the free feeling of going as fast as the chair would take me.

The opportunities given to me in middle school sports were where I realized what I could do and how I could use sports to level the playing field. It was there that people focused on what I could do rather than my limitations. It was a great time in my life, and it taught me a lot, not only about being competitive, but also about how to be successful with the help of other people.

14 Rolling From Middle School to High School

Ask any kid about the most difficult time he or she had in school. Many will tell you it is the transition from middle school to high school that is most difficult. Like most other kids, I had the same challenge, but mine was for different reasons. When we were young, most of my friends had the same interests as I did. We were all about just hanging out and having fun. As my friends got older, their interests turned to girls and other social activities. After reaching high school, they were able to get their driver's licenses and enjoy going wherever they wanted.

I chose not to dwell on things I was unable to do and instead focused on things I could. With that in mind, I turned once again to what I knew best growing up—my true passion, athletics. Although there are wheelchair sports at the high school level, I decided to change my focus from playing sports to managing and coaching.

Over my next four years of school, I was able to be part of both the football and basketball programs. Thankfully for me, I was able to be part of the boys' varsity basketball team with my older brother, and I assisted in coaching my younger brother as he was growing up.

There's no doubt that being involved in these activities made my transition from middle to high school easier. Not only was I just one of the guys, but there was also no mention of my having a disability when on the court or the field. For me, my focus was on doing my best and serving in any role I could to positively impact my teammates and those around me. Another aspect that made my transition easier was the fact that, although my role may have changed from player to manager, my expectations remained the same.

15

The Bomber Brotherhood

In chapter one, I began with the story of how I reached the mountaintop of college hoops by winning two national championships. Though that was the start of this book, that wasn't the start of my journey with hoops.

None of this would have been possible without Kohler High School's basketball coaches, who gave me the opportunity to be part of the program. Coach Jeff Wolf took me under his wing for two years. He gave me the opportunity to manage as well as give input. Coach Wolf graduated from Kohler back in the 1970s. After high school, he played for the University of North Carolina, and he played for several years professionally overseas. His expertise taught me a great deal before he moved on after my sophomore year.

Next came Coach Ken Roeder. Coach Roeder definitely brought a new intensity level to the program. I really enjoyed having him coach, as he was also a teacher at the school, so I could go into his class and talk about the team.

Along with Coach Roeder came Coach Kyle Gebler. Coach Gebler was the coach who kept everything loose. When I was running the clock, he usually came over to joke about something going on in practice. The constant under both Coach Wolf and Coach Roeder was JV/assistant varsity coach Larry Kampman (Kampy). He was great to be around. Running the half-court challenge after practice (the first player to make half-court shot somehow found a couple dollars on the floor) remained a tradition until he passed away a few years back. Kampy was my dad's high school JV basketball coach, too. I enjoyed the stories he told about my dad's teams.

I loved being part of the game at a school of 140 kids, playing at the Kohler High School gym in front of my friends, family, and the Kohler community.

My sophomore and junior years in high school, which I spent with the basketball team alongside my brothers, were some of the greatest times I ever had. My little brother Dominic was the ball boy, and Douglas was playing varsity.

My two fondest memories from those years happened my junior and senior years. My second favorite memory was during my senior year, when I will never forget my cousin Michael carrying me through the banner as I was introduced as part of the starting lineup on Senior Night. I never played a minute or got into a game, but I was part of my home team and took to the court with my teammates. That senior night against Cedar Grove didn't go our way, but the results didn't matter. It was the ride that took place before the game that I will always remember.

My fondest memory during those two seasons was during my junior year and Douglas's senior year, when we went up against Sheboygan Falls. It seems like only yesterday we were playing against our neighboring school, Sheboygan Falls, the night before we started Christmas break. Sheboygan Falls was a much larger school than we were, but due to their proximity, we were neighborhood rivals.

What made things more interesting for the Bocchini family was that Mom was the assistant to the athletic director (AD) at Sheboygan Falls. Trailing all night long, we came back to tie things up at the end of regulation play, putting the game into overtime. Falls quickly took the lead in overtime and worked hard to hold us off. Down by two with under fifteen seconds, we needed to foul in hopes of having one last chance. Falls missed the front of end of the bonus, giving us one last shot. After we missed a shot to tie the game, the ball was tipped out to my brother at the three-point line. With no hesitation, Douglas launched a three. As time expired, the ball went through the net—game over! It was our first win over Falls in years. After the game, my mother was asked what she was thinking when Douglas got the ball. Her response was, "Don't shoot." I am glad he didn't listen to her.

The best part wasn't that we won, although that felt pretty good. It was the fact that the night was a big moment for our family and probably my best moment as a Kohler Bomber.

As I look back on my time at Kohler, I may not remember all the wins and losses. However, I do remember our family and all the memories that were made together.

Those two seasons I got to spend with my brothers were probably the most fun I had in the game at any level. Championships are all good, but there is nothing quite like game time in your hometown, in front of your friends and family.

If you take anything from these stories, take this. Never forget where you come from in the pursuit of where you are going. Never forget the people who started you on the path you are on today. In my case, never forget the place you were when you saw your older brother hit the game winner, only to go to McDonald's to hear the cashier say, "No Bocchinis allowed." That voice was the voice of the Sheboygan Falls Falcons announcer, who called the game when Douglas took it home!

16 Rolling Like Rudy

I have talked about some of the athletics opportunities I've been fortunate enough to have and their huge impact on my life. While many of them happened on the hardwood of a gymnasium, that wasn't the only platform that provided me with great moments on the playing field. Football gave me the opportunity to meet some of my best friends, gave me some of my greatest memories, and one night, offered me the personal highlight of my high school athletic career.

Growing up in the small Village of Kohler, Wisconsin, my middle school football career was full of moments that I'll never forget. However, when I was in eighth grade, it seemed as though my football career would end. I would not be able to play in high school, not only because of my disability, but also because Kohler didn't have enough football players to field a team on its own.

As winter rolled around, I remember sitting at a basketball

game with my dad. We were playing one of our rivals, Sheboygan Lutheran. Proximity-wise, the schools were very close, and many of the kids knew each other. As we were watching the game, Lutheran's athletic director/football coach Al Holzheimer approached my dad to say they were looking at creating a co-op football team between Lutheran and Kohler the following year. The realization that football was going to be back for my high school career and that Friday nights were going to be fun again was really exciting.

For my next four years, the two schools came together under one team. We became a brotherhood, a family. Coaches Matt Zavada, Holzheimer, and Frantz, as well as all the other coaches, worked us hard but always made it fun. We didn't win a lot of games, but to us, that wasn't what it was about. It was about playing our tails off for one another and forming the bonds that will never be forgotten. Although we didn't create a great number of highlights on the scoreboard, there is one highlight of my career, during my senior year, that I will never forget.

I was sitting in a computer class when my teacher, Mrs. Jodi Grossen, asked us to pull up a website. It was the Rudy Award website. The Rudy Award is a national award given to a high school football player or manager who exemplifies courage and strength as he inspires his team on the field—all while overcoming adversity. To be eligible for this award, you have to be nominated by one of your coaches and submitted for nomination. Without my knowing, Head Coach Matt Zavada had nominated me for the national award.

To earn the award, you needed to receive votes by the clicks you received on your profile on their website. As I said earlier, one of the coolest parts of our co-op was a closeness of our program. This was evident throughout my career, but never more so than after the football season that year. Watching me receive thousands of votes from so many friends was humbling.

No, I did not win the national Rudy award and the $10,000 scholarship that comes with it. Instead, one evening, I received something much more meaningful, much more than I could have ever dreamt. Kohler and Sheboygan Lutheran were playing against each other in basketball at the Kohler gym. As the JV game ended and the varsity players got ready to hit the court for warmups, the announcer called everyone to attention, called me to center court, and asked my family to come out with me. When I looked up in the stands, I noticed that the gym was packed. I saw all of my family there—not just my family and grandparents, but my teammates/brothers from the team, and what seemed to be the entire student body from both schools. Even my good friend and teammate Kurt Stielow came back from college to be there for me. I didn't realize how many people supported me along the way in hopes of pushing for me to win the national award.

This event and ceremony had been kept a secret from both my parents and me. If you know anything about Kohler, it is not easy to keep a secret. I remember going to center court when my name was called and looking around the gym, with both sides' spectators standing, thinking to myself, *Wow, this is unreal. I can't believe people felt like I made this type of impact.* At that time, they presented me with my own Rudy Award and a scholarship created for me by all these generous friends. No time in my life ever felt so good.

That night was not just about being given the award. It was about being part of the brotherhood of the two schools and the impact we had on these two communities. I'm proud to say the team created a Rudy Award given to one of the players on the team.

To this day, it is still difficult for me to realize that I made such an impact during my four years. It was truly special. Personally, this award gave me the confidence and realization that I was fortunate enough to impact others around me. Not a day goes by in my life that I don't try to live up to the Rudy Award standards of courage, strength, and inspiring others around me.

17

From Hometown to Second Home

Ask any high school senior what they are looking most forward to, and most will tell you the same thing: "I can't wait for June and graduation." Then when June comes, most of them will be thinking, *Now what?* Many of them have been planning for months, if not years, for the "now what," but all of a sudden, reality sets in.

That was the case for me in June, 2010. Graduation was here, and I was pumped to start a new chapter of my life. At the same time, I was pretty nervous. I would be heading off to Whitewater in the fall, and at this point, I had not been that far from home regularly.

Picture a kid whose parents have helped him with daily tasks for his entire life; you can understand my trepidation. I wouldn't call it fear, because I wasn't scared. I was more nervous because this was the first chance I had to be on my own. This also meant figuring things out on my own to be successful.

The most difficult part of this transition came early. At the end of my senior year of high school, my parents and I decided it would be best for me to take a summer transition course offered through UW–Whitewater. It allowed students who not only had physical but also academic challenges to take a month-long course, making sure they were ready for college life and the university was ready for them.

I loved Whitewater and my college career, but to say the beginning was easy would be a complete lie. I was a small-town kid with very strong ties to his hometown. I can still remember about a week into the transition course, texting my parents saying, "I'm not cut out for this; I want to come home." This is when my parents gave me a choice. "You can come home and live with us for the rest of your life, or you can stick it out. It's up to you." Some people might think this seems a bit harsh, but you need to understand the house I grew up in to know what they're saying. Instead of letting me take the easy way out and come home, they were basically saying, "We didn't place limitations on you early in life; it is now time for you to grow up, develop yourself, and show everyone you can do this."

When the fall classes began, I struggled. Not on the academic end, but definitely socially. The one thing I knew is that I wasn't happy. I missed being home. I missed being part of a team, being around the guys. I missed sports. I missed the one thing I loved the most and felt most passionate about because it allowed others to not see my disability.

It wasn't until around Thanksgiving that I realized I needed to figure it out. I had to try again to be part of a program and a team. I remember calling my parents and saying, "Mom, Dad, would you mind if I joined the basketball program or found something in athletics to be part of?"

My dad responded, "That would be great, as long as your grades don't slip." A smile broke out on my face; I knew that wasn't going to be a problem. If I got involved in something, it would help me focus academically and make friends socially. From that point forward, instead of viewing being away from home as a negative, I viewed it as a positive and a chance to make my parents and family very proud. Now I just needed to figure out how I was going to get there.

18

The Encounter That Changed My Life

Coming back for the second semester of my freshman year was not easy. Although before break, I started to talk to people about getting involved in athletics, nothing had yet materialized. I wasn't sure what to do.

A few weeks into the semester, my dad called me to see if I wanted to come home for the weekend. He told me on the way home that we were going to stop in the Milwaukee area to watch Matt, the son of Dad's grade school friend Jim Krueger, play basketball for Franklin High School. Franklin was playing Kenosha Bradford for the conference championship. Matt was a smooth lefty who could shoot the jump shot but also take the ball to the basket. What I didn't know was that Matt was being recruited by a variety of colleges in Wisconsin to play basketball, and several coaches were in the stands that evening. As the game started, Mr. Krueger was telling us about Bradford's top player, Quardell

Young. Mr. Krueger coached Matt and Quardell during the summer on the AAU circuit. I watched intently as the action between Kenosha Bradford and Franklin became a really outstanding basketball game. Franklin ended up winning, but that's not what I remember most about that night.

After the game, we hung around the gym with Mr. and Mrs. Krueger to catch Matt and congratulate him on the win. There were several coaches with Mr. Krueger, as they were interested in Matt and his intentions for the following year. I looked up as one of the coaches approached me and said, "Hey, man, I like your shirt." I was wearing my UW–Whitewater shirt. He then introduced himself as Coach Miller, the men's basketball coach at University of Wisconsin–Whitewater. I wasn't sure what to say. "Any thoughts on making it to the NCAA tourney? How does the team look for next year?" Finally, all that came out was, "Do you need any help next year?" He looked a little surprised, but then said, "Stop by my office in the fall and we will discuss it."

Throughout the spring of my freshman year, I knew I had something to look forward to in the fall. That short meeting with coach Miller that night would change my life forever, giving me an opportunity that I would take and never look back.

19

Friendships and So Much More

In the fall of my sophomore year, I enrolled in Coach Miller's class, Coaching Basketball, in hopes of getting closer to some of the athletes and the program. I remember it was mid-October and class had just ended when Coach Miller looked at me and asked, "Are you coming to practice today?"

"You want me to?" I replied.

"You want to be part of the team?" Coach answered. That day, at 2:30, I showed up at my first practice.

As you can imagine, I was nervous as all get out. I had not been part of a basketball team for over a year, and college ball would be at a whole different level than Kohler High School had been. As I went around the gym, several guys came up to me and introduced themselves. The first one was Chris Davis, later that year named National Player of the Year 2012. Next was Luke Knoble, then Eric Bryson. While all the guys made me feel welcome, there was one encounter that stuck out above the rest because of the impact he would later make in my life. Cody Odegard, a sophomore guard out of Poynette, Wisconsin, came up to me and said, "What's up, man?" greetings much like the others had. Then, at the end of practice, I felt a hand on my shoulder. I turned my head, and it was Cody. It was almost as if he were saying, "Welcome to the team. This is your team, too." I went home after practice fired up. I now felt like part of the family. Little did I realize at the time how special my relationship with Cody and this team would become.

20 Embrace the Grind

By now, you no doubt can see my love for sports, but I have to admit that the seasons did get long at times. Because I started at such a young age, though, I had learned to embrace the grind that comes with athletics and the opportunity to level the playing field through the use of sports. There was one grind, however, that I wasn't anxious to embrace. That was therapy.

While most kids' after-school schedules included activities like piano lessons, play practice, athletics, or studying—all things that would make them better through their lives—my afternoons included going to physical therapy. Growing up, I knew going to therapy was a part of life, part of having CP, part of the grind. What I did not understand at the time was its importance to me, why I should embrace it, and how it was going to make me better in the long term.

One of the effects of cerebral palsy is very high muscle tone. In my case, it was in my legs and my arms. I struggled to turn my palms up and straighten my legs. From when I was one year old and all through my life, my therapy has focused on reducing that muscle tone.

When I was smaller, I was able to walk with a walker. Due to the high tone, my legs wanted to cross over when I was walking. I spent many hours practicing my gait while holding onto parallel bars. My physical therapist, Brenda Schilder, spent much of our time together laying on the floor holding on to my legs, keeping them in line, not allowing them to cross. She would say it was such good exercise for her as well, because she continually worked up a sweat!

Other days, I would have two therapists working with me at the same time. One therapist would sit behind me on a big bolster that stretched my hamstrings, working my core and strengthening my muscles to help me sit up tall. All of this happened while the occupational therapist worked in front of me. She focused on breaking down the tone in my arms and teaching me how to turn my palms face up. This was accomplished with stretching and deep massages to soften the muscles so they would become nice and extended. The therapists' goal was to teach my muscles how they should be—long and loose. This was called muscle memory.

I would like to say I was the ideal client, but I can't. Fortunately for me, they really didn't care whether I wanted to be there. As a matter of fact, neither did my mom. Looking back, I am really grateful for all of them: Brenda Schilder, Lori Schad, Gail Slaughter, Wendy Arthur and Karen Cowdy, just to name a few. Their putting up with my arguing and complaining helped me get to where I am today. Sometimes it is good when you don't win an argument.

It wasn't until high school that I stopped looking at therapy as a grind and instead embraced it more as a challenge, like an athlete does at practice. All that work I did when I was young carried over to the opportunities I would face in college. I finally understood therapy as a way to better myself so I could succeed at school and prepare to live alone.

When I got to Whitewater, I met Mike Lenzer, the university's physical therapist. Mike continued my therapy, driving me harder than ever before and helping me improve physically.

After my sophomore year, my first season with the men's basketball team, I decided to continue what Mike and I worked so hard to accomplish.

I was heading home for the summer and knew I couldn't go back to school the following fall having lost the progress we had made because I took the summer off. I went back to work with Brenda, this time focusing on what I needed to succeed as an adult and realizing the benefit of continual therapy and exercise.

What I learned through all this is that there will be moments in your life when the grind seems too much and it is difficult to believe it has a purpose. It is at these times that you need to realize this: Don't skip that step. Don't cheat the process. Keep pushing behind the scenes. When there are no fans in the gym, when there isn't a crowd, when you all alone in the office, when you do it just for yourself . . . that's the greatest feeling in the world.

21   My Second Family

For the next five years, my life was consumed with college and basketball and the friends/caregivers that made it all possible. Some of the greatest highlights of my college career will never make it to film, but they'll stick with me forever.

Often, I talk about my successes athletically or academically. One major factor may have gone unnoticed. I had a group of people whom I needed to achieve my goals. They were there for my day-to-day tasks. Some would call them caregivers, but I saw them as my friends who then became my family. I could focus on the big things in my life because they took care of the little things. One of these caregivers was Cody, my friend and teammate. In addition to Cody, a group of people watched out for me and became my second family. I met my second family in a variety of ways. Some were caregivers who became friends over the course of time, and others I met through my involvement with the basketball program or through mutual friends. They included Eric, Calvin, Josh, Jaz, Ben, Tony, Asa, Cheryl, Taylor, Simone, Jordie, Abbie, Dylan, Kaitlin, and Philly. Without them, I wouldn't have made it. They made life so much easier. These guys always made sure I was taken care of, whether it was helping me complete homework during tutor sessions, covering shifts for me daily, or just stepping up and being there for me as friends. This group made a world of difference in my life.

One thing this group did not do was view me as disabled or allow me to see myself that way. I truly appreciated being surrounded by friends who got beyond the chair to see me and allow me to do some pretty special things. To them, there was no CP—there was just AJ.

You may be saying, "That's great for you, but what does this have to do with me?" The answer is simple. None of the people I refer to as my second family are blood relatives. They are a group of friends who made sacrifices and created a bond that has lasted much longer than the short time in which it was formed. Please open yourself up to finding that second family. Look for that support system that can become so much more.

22 MY LONGEST SUMMER: The Bumpy Road to the Whitewater FINISH Line

When most kids head home from college for the summer, they have big plans, like hanging with friends, going to sporting events and concerts, and engaging in other fun activities. I was no different.

I had just gotten a new seat for my chair. It helped me to sit up taller, and I was ready to rock 'n' roll. Over the course of the last month of the semester, I had been adjusting to the new seat, and I loved it. My posture was good, and so was school.

When I got home for the summer, I was excited to put my sweatshirts away. It was T-shirts and shorts time. Things were good. Or so I thought. One day while I was going to bed, I realized the back of my shoulder hurt. My parents put a bandage on it, and I went to bed. I thought nothing of it; it was just a scrape. Unfortunately, it turned out to be much more. I woke up the next day and was getting dressed when my dad looked at it again and realized this was not just a scrape. My new seat had been irritating my shoulder, so off to the doctor's office we went. When I arrived, the nurse told me I had an infection but wasn't exactly sure what it was. Then the doctor came in and advised us that it was MRSA, which is an extremely contagious staph infection.

This could not have happened at a worse time. I was in graduate school and planning to take a summer course starting in July, allowing me to graduate the following spring. My Baclofen pump, which is needed to loosen my muscle tone, also needed replacing this summer, as it was seven years old. That surgery was scheduled for early July.

The summer of rocking 'n' rolling stopped in an instant. To make matters even worse, I was no longer allowed in my chair because it could reaggravate the wound.

As you can imagine, not being able to take a summer class or have surgery as scheduled is one thing, but not being able to drive my chair and get from point A to point B by myself was devastating. On top of that, most of my friends were scheduled to graduate in the spring of 2016, and I was concerned that my inability to take a summer course would impact my ability not only to graduate the following spring, but also to go back to school and see all my friends for the last year together.

I was completely unsure of myself and didn't know where to go next. I had many visitors that summer who helped me get through this time. My brothers Dominic and Douglas and our friend Casey, who came to visit most of the summer, were there whenever I needed them. This allowed my parents the freedom to go to work and make sure everything was taken care of.

While my family and my local friends were around, I longed for the days of Whitewater. Despite all of the issues that the summer had brought, it was still my goal to get back there. One day, while I was lying on the couch watching TV, I received a text from UW–Whitewater, Assistant Coach Reid Gibbs (Coach G). The text said, "Little bro, what are you doing?"

I responded with, "Nothing coach. I have a bum shoulder, and it's frustrating as heck because I can't get out and do anything." He didn't respond for a little while, and I began to get sad. Then I realized Coach G was standing at my door. He had driven all the way from Whitewater just to check up on me. We talked about everything—the team, the basketball program, and just life in general. When I looked up to the ceiling as he left, I thought to myself, *I'm going to be all right. This is going to heal, and I'm going back to school to finish my master's.*

Later that summer, my MRSA had cleared up, or so I thought. Then it came back, but this time I was not as devastated. The doctor advised me that the infection wasn't as bad as the first time around, and I could still have my surgery for my Baclofen pump. After a tough eight weeks, surgery was over, and my bouts with MRSA were gone. No more lying on the couch, no more sponge baths. I was able to shower. I was on the road to recovery.

But another accident was just around the corner. I slipped in the shower and busted some teeth. We took an emergency run to the dentist's office (here we go again), but the office was closed. Thankfully, Dad knew Doctor Hess and his wife Sara pretty well. Dad made a quick call and found Mrs. Hess. She was able to find Dr. Hess rapidly, and he could do the emergency work. I thought to myself, *Man, am I ever going to get out of the woods*? I again started to wonder if I were going to get a chance to go back to school. Thankfully, Doctor Hess was able to do some great work. After a few visits, I was back up and on the run. I couldn't wait to get back to Whitewater for the fall semester.

What drove me that summer was my family who took care of me and all of my friends who were counting on me to get back and finish what we started together. I wanted to be able to walk across the stage together as we planned. When I would post updates on how I was doing, my friends continued to encourage me, knowing I would get back. Without everyone's support, I would never have made it back, and I wouldn't have a master's degree.

That summer taught me so much about myself and the people around me. No matter what happens, you can always make it. Nobody is going to remember exactly what obstacles you faced, but they will remember how you handled yourself when adversity stared you in the face. Instead of running around or avoiding adversities, face them head on and run right through them.

I could have given up, but I didn't. My family, friends, teammates, coaches, and professors were supportive of me and understanding of what I was going through. That's what made the reward of going back to school that fall so special—no one allowed me to let a few setbacks derail my journey toward the Whitewater FINISH line.

23   Life After College

I graduated in 2016 with my master's in athletic administration. I headed home with hopes of getting a job right away. As with many recent graduates, that didn't happen. I spent the summer sending out resumes and following them up. Life wasn't all bad, as my parents lived in Elkhart Lake, and often you'd find me at the Ostoff Resort, enjoying the view of the lake.

In August, I headed to the Racine/Kenosha area to pursue my next step in life, coaching at Saint Catherine's in Racine, with Coach Nick Bennett. I had met Nick at UW–Whitewater during my days as student manager. As the season didn't start until November, I was able to get a job at the Kenosha YMCA helping with the Miracle League T-ball league for kids with special needs. It was great.

Back to Coach Bennett and Saint Catherine's. Nick had been the head assistant at Whitewater for three years, including during our second national championship season. Nick decided to finish his master's at UWW and start teaching. Many of you who know the basketball circles in Wisconsin may recognize the last name. Nick is the son of the legendary Coach Jack Bennett of UW–Stevens Point; the nephew of Dick Bennett, long-time coach at UW–Madison; and the cousin of Tony Bennett, head coach of University of Virginia. It was an honor for me to be able to coach with Nick.

Beyond Coach Bennett, Pat Souter was also on our staff. I knew Pat as a player and good friend from our second national championship team at Whitewater.

My only challenge now was how to get to practice every day and to games on game nights. That is when Mike Rittgers stepped in. Mike was not only an assistant coach at St. Cat's, but also an alumnus. Mike picked me up every day, driving me to practices and games using my van.

As for St. Cat's, it is a very old school. The gym was on the second floor, and the school had no passenger elevators. What it did have was a small maintenance elevator, not large enough for my power wheelchair. Mike and I would take my manual chair, cram into the elevator, and go up to the gym for practice. We were always thankful when we successfully made it back down.

The cool thing about having my manual chair in the gym is that the coaches would always make me work out like the rest of the team. After practice was over, my workout was rolling my chair up and down the floor, pushing the wheels with all the arm strength I had.

I would be totally remiss if I didn't mention the Saint Cat's athletic director, John Johnson. I had known of John for years. John had a son, Brady, who also had cerebral palsy. In Brady's case, the CP was much more severe than mine, and he had passed away several years earlier.

John allowed coach Bennett to hire me and made sure I was always taken care of. Coaching at St. Cat's was like a dream come true. However, I couldn't have done it if Coach Bennett and John had not taken a chance on me. I also wouldn't have made such a good friend in Mike, and without his help, I wouldn't have had my first varsity boys' basketball coaching job. At no time in my life have I felt more fortunate to have "family" in my life . . . my family from UWW, and my new family from Saint Catherine's.

FINISH
The Meaning

Family First

No LImitations

Never Quit

Make an Impact

Surround Yourself With Great People

Help Others

25

FINISH
Family First

The letter F in FINISH stands for **FAMILY** first. Family is the most important thing you have. There are many different ways to define family. Family might mean the people in your household, like your mom and dad, brothers or sisters, aunts, uncles, cousins, or neighbors. Or, family may go well beyond this and is often found when you are not looking. For me, family includes my friends at Whitewater, who took me to parties and events by driving me and carrying me up and down steps. It includes my aides and therapists, without whom I would have never made it through school. It includes my coaches and teammates, who not only helped me transition to my new role, but also helped me become a leader.

Without my entire family, I wouldn't be here, and there's no doubt in my mind I wouldn't be sharing my story in hopes of helping others. Family is the most important thing you are going to have in your life. Your records, accolades, and accomplishments will fade in time, but your family will always be there to support you in the pursuit of your goals. It's okay to lean on them and ask for help when times get tough. I did, and that's how I got here. It's also okay to ask for advice when you need it. Your family is there to help you through difficult situations or challenges. Lean on the people you trust, and you will find the true definition of family. In turn, you'll achieve your goals with their support.

26

FINISH
No Limitations

The first I in FINISH stands for the I in the word limitations, or in my case **NO LIMITATIONS**. Yes, I was born with CP. Yes, I had challenges. We all have challenges in life, but that does not mean we have limitations.

One of the greatest things family (parents, relatives, friends, teachers, and coaches) ever did for me was place no limitations on what I could do. Everyone in my life has found a way to put me in a position to be successful.

That is the key to no limitations. You have to always find a way to make yourself successful. Regardless of what you're going through, set your goals high and remember to fall back on the letter F (FAMILY) if you come up short. They will always be there to help you get back on the horse.

If people had placed limits on me early in life, I would not have ended up with a master's degree and living an independent life.

I most certainly wouldn't be writing this book today, either. It is only because my family refused to place limitations on me, and I refused to limit myself, that I'm in the position I am today.

A no-limitations attitude will knock down the roadblocks in front of you. A no-limitations attitude will allow you to reach your goals, set new ones, and keep climbing. A no-limitations attitude will help others around you be successful as your attitude becomes contagious. I'll leave you with this thought: in NO LIMITATIONS, there's no such thing as a backward step. Backward steps only exist when you place limitations on what you can do. And always remember this: place no limitations on yourself to FINISH your goals.

27

FINISH
Never Quit

N is for **NEVER QUIT**. In life and in pursuit of your goals, you're going to face adversity. That's just how life works. I know at times it gets tough. I can't tell you how many times there have been days I just wanted to quit and give up on my pursuit and settle for just being average. Then I would think to myself, *I can't do that.* There are too many people who have worked too hard to help me get in the position I am today. My mom put in countless hours to take me to PT so I could get stronger. My brothers have been there for me every step of the way. My dad inspired my passion for athletics, which led to my career path, and all the rest of my FAMILY pushed me every step of the way. If we quit on ourselves, then we are really quitting on somebody else who may have helped us or may be inspired by us.

There were countless times in my journey—after surgery, a caregiver issue, or a therapy session—when I thought to myself, *Is this really the right thing to do? Maybe I should just quit.* Then something would click. I'd remember that nothing I do is just about me. It's about setting an example for others. I will never give up on my dreams, my hopes of achieving my goals, and my commitment to helping others realize that it's possible to achieve theirs.

If I quit, everything we accomplished together goes out the window and means nothing. No matter how much adversity you face, no matter how many times you get knocked down, don't quit. NEVER QUIT. Nothing is ever easy in the pursuit of success and dreams.

28

FINISH
Make an Impact

The second I in FINISH is for **IMPACT**, as in Make an Impact. This is possibly the most important opportunity you have in life. Will your impact be positive? It is your choice. We will be judged on how we handle opportunities to make an impact. Regardless of your situation, everyone has a platform, and with that comes an opportunity to make a positive impact on others. The cool thing is that you never know how your attitude might help someone else.

I view my CP as my platform. It presents me with some physical challenges, no doubt, but instead of dwelling on the challenges, I choose to take a different route that I hope to pass on to you. CP allows me to show others what is possible regardless of what obstacles present themselves. When I was younger, I had what I call the "me mentality." I thought I had to do everything in my power to make myself and only myself a success. Now I see my success as more about how I can make a positive impact on others.

The point of this chapter isn't about me. It's about you. No matter how big or how small you are, no matter your age, no matter what your situation is, everyone has an opportunity to make a positive impact on others. If someone is having a rough day, pick them up with a smile and give them positive encouragement. Your success is often based on how you treat others, whether they are family, friends, or strangers. Your attitude toward life sets an example.

I challenge you to take five minutes and write down a list of the opportunities you have to make a difference in the lives of others. Then, go out and make an impact. It is not about the visibility of what you do. It's about the difference you make in the lives of others, helping them become successful so they may achieve their goals.

Let me leave you with the following thought, regardless of whether you play a sport, teach kids, or work hard every day in any other type of job. The day you retire, your uniform will be hung up, and your accomplishments will fade, but the positive impact you had on others will last forever.

FINISH
Surround Yourself With Great People

29

S is for **SURROUND yourself with great people**. Your team makes all the difference.

Many people over the course of the last few years have asked me: "AJ, how did you do it? How did you overcome your challenges to achieve what you have?" I'll be the first to tell you that the key to my success was not about me but about the people around me.

I've been fortunate enough to have people in my life who believed in me. It started with my parents and relatives and has continued with the people I choose to put in my life and those who choose to include me in theirs. If you surround yourself with great people, chances are they will share and support your vision of where you see yourself. In turn, they will do everything in their power to assist you in being successful in pursuing your dreams.

The journey toward your goals is no doubt going to have peaks and valleys, highs and lows, but that's okay. Make sure you have people who will help you through the journey. Once you achieve your goal, they will help you to the next one.

Regardless of age, challenge, or what you are going through in life, we all have those people we can lean on who we know will help us get where we want to be.

30

FINISH
Help Others

The final letter H is for **HELP OTHERS**. Don't just chase your own dreams; help others chase theirs. This is possibly the most important letter of my definition of FINISH. We are all given a platform, an opportunity to chase our dreams and successes. This is great, but eventually our dreams and successes will present us other opportunities to help others be successful, to help others achieve their dreams.

Yes, I was born two months prematurely, weighing 3 lbs. 14 oz. Yes, I have cerebral palsy. Early in life, I was unsure what life would be like. Although a challenge, my life has also presented me with an opportunity to help others who may be fighting a different battle or a different situation.

Over the course of defining FINISH, I showed you my keys to success: family, no limitations, never quitting, impacting others, surrounding yourself with great people, and helping others. If you keep these in mind, you will put yourself in a great position to not only follow your dreams, but to help others do the same.

I wrote this book not for personal gain or glory. I wrote it to help others see what is possible. I hope I have helped you realize that regardless of what you are going through, regardless of where you are in life, there's always an opportunity to put yourself aside and help someone else achieve their vision and their dreams. If you do this, I promise you will feel great, because you will be a part of their success. You will help them FINISH.

31 UNFINISHED BUSINESSS
Final Chapter

Throughout these pages, I have truly enjoyed sharing my story with you regarding the first twenty-six years of my life. Or, as I like to call it, my first quarter of the game of life. I can only hope that you have enjoyed reading it as much as I have enjoyed writing it.

While this book may have concluded, I want to make one last thing perfectly clear. Through the ups and downs, the highs and lows, the CP, the championships, and the master's degree, one thing is for certain. My journey is unfinished. I'm just getting started, and that's the mentality I want every single one of you to take with you. You always have unfinished business. Life never stops. The game keeps going.

When you have a setback, I hope you think of FINISH and how it can impact you:

Put FAMILY first

NO LIMITATIONS

NEVER quit

Make an IMPACT

SURROUND yourself with great people

HELP others

It has been a true joy of mine to share my story with you, and it is my sincere hope that you are able to take even some of what you learned about me and apply it to your life to make yourself and others around you successful. No matter what happens in your life, always remember to FINISH what you started. Now go out, tip over, tear out a milk machine, drive into a lake, and fall off a curb—it's okay! It's all part of learning how to FINISH.

ACKNOWLEDGMENTS
More Than Coaches and Staff

Earlier, I talked about a chance encounter with University of Wisconsin–Whitewater coach Pat Miller during a high school basketball game in Franklin, Wisconsin. This encounter helped jumpstart my success as a student/manager for the UW–Whitewater men's basketball team, eventually leading us toward two national championships.

Those magical moments would not have been possible without the impact of a special group of people who turned a small-town kid into a leader over the course of six years in undergraduate and then graduate school. These were the coaches and staff at the University of Wisconsin–Whitewater.

In the fall 2012, Coach Miller took a big risk by taking on a kid from Kohler and giving me an opportunity to be a part of the big stage of Division III basketball. My introduction to Coach Miller was just the start of great relationships I formed with the coaches over the course of my college career.

I consider 2012 the hype man year. That season, I was introduced to assistant coaches Lou Chapman, Dick Luther, Paul Griffin, and Kai Instaford, along with fellow student assistant Jake Gritzmacher (Gritz). These guys were great to work with, and each had an impact on my life in a different way.

Lou took me under his wing almost immediately and got me psyched for practices and games. He always said my responsibility was to be the hype man who gets the guys ready to play every day. Coach Luther gave me wisdom and served as a great mentor. No matter what happened, I could always learn something from Coach, not just about the game but about life itself.

Paul was always there to help me. Many stories stuck with me during this season, but I will always remember one in particular about Paul. My mom, my aunt, and I had just arrived in Salem, Virginia, prior to the semifinal game of the 2012 Final Four. As we arrived at the Civic Center, I got out of the van thinking, "Where do I go now?" As I came out, Paul was standing there, waiting to take me to the locker room and join the team in pregame.

Kai and Jake took me under their wings and taught me how to be a manager at the college level. It wasn't always easy on them, as I made many rookie mistakes, but they always pointed me in the right direction.

If not for this great staff, no doubt 2012, my future at UWW, and my story would have been completely different.

After the 2012 season, Coach Luther departed, while all other staff remained. New to the coaching staff would be Reid Gibbs. Reid and I instantly forged a great relationship. Reid not only helped me on the court but was also my go-to person during graduate school. No doubt I would have never been able to get through that last year and a half without his help.

Following the 2013 season, Coaches Lou, Paul, and Gritz decided to move on. This was definitely bittersweet, as we had two great years together; however, Coaches Miller, Gibbs, and Kai remained.

New to the staff were Nick Bennett, Kyle Heikenen, and Wes Bertram. Coach Bennett had a great basketball mind, having won a national championship as a player at University of Wisconsin–Stevens Point and having been an assistant in a couple of men's Division I basketball programs. Kyle and Wes always looked out for me during our time together. This was a special group who came together for our second national championship in three years.

Each of these coaches and staff affected me not only as a team member but as a person. They gave a kid from a small town a chance, helping him grow into a man by the time he was done with college. For that, I am very grateful and appreciative.

I would be remiss to not mention two other staff members who were instrumental at UWW during my graduate school career: Dr. Kristina Navarro and Dr. Kelly Witte. Kristina, the leader of the higher education and leadership program, helped me with the process and paperwork to get into the athletic administration master's program, and she guided me every step of the way. Kelly was my first professor in the graduate program. She inspired me and drove me to continue when I wasn't sure grad school was right for me

Without all these people, I would not be where I am now. I would not have the memories and friendships that remain with me to this day. They allowed me to FINISH the first quarter of my life.

ACKNOWLEDGMENTS
Unknown Heroes

I have touched on many memories and opportunities that have helped me get to where I am now. Those experiences were filled with many great people. I would be remiss if I didn't share some of them with you.

When I was the ripe young ages of eight months to three years old, my therapists were Lori Schad, Gail Slaughter, Wendy Arthur, and Linda Kleiban. It was fun because it was play. They were the first people who taught my body how it should work.

As you may recall, Brenda Schilder and Karen Cowdy were my therapists as I got older. They learned to modify my therapy sessions to relate to what was needed for me to succeed as a young adult. They made sure my sessions were something I could apply long term in my life.

Lightfoot was where I spent my first years at school. There,

I was introduced to Fred Brown, the special education gym teacher. What I remember most was swimming a couple days each week. No matter how much he tried, no matter what flotation device he created, I always ended up floating face down. Thanks for always being there to turn me face up, Mr. Brown!

In Kohler Elementary School, my teachers were Mrs. Braatz, Mrs. Wolfert, Mrs. Schinabeck, Mrs. Halverson, Mrs. LaDuke, Mr. DuMez, and Mr. Hucke—to name a few. I was just another kid in the classroom. They didn't see my chair, except during those times when I tore up the door frames going in and out. This extended to my classmates, too. The story goes that when a new kid came into the classroom, he pointed to me and asked, "Who is that?" My classmates replied, "Oh, that's just AJ."

Mr. Richards was my gym teacher. He took me to the Sports Core to sit in the hot tub and loosen up my muscles. It was great for me, and I don't believe he minded hanging out in a hot tub either.

Jodi Wagner and Kelly Dirkse worked hard to make sure I had what I needed in and out of the classroom to succeed.

But I have to say Kohler School would not have meant as

much to me and I wouldn't have been so successful if it weren't for Mrs. Dexheimer (Mrs. D). She came into my life when I was in 4K (four-year-old kindergarten), and we stuck together for ten years. With her, I learned that I could do anything. She taught me that it was important to know how to laugh—not only at yourself, but at life in general. She made sure I understood that making people smile was a great gift.

Carol Harpold was not only a therapist at Kohler School, but she also had a son from Oostburg who played soccer against my older brother, Douglas. Along the sidelines at those games, she introduced me to the idea of a standing wheelchair and voice recognition software. Without those, I would not have had the experiences I did.

With my standing wheelchair, I was able to stand at half court during warmups, giving high fives to my teammates. This became very important to me because they no longer had to lean down; I was already on their level. To say the voice recognition software gave me new opportunity would be an understatement. Without it, I would not have been able to write this book.

Lori Schmid was my case manager at Kohler School; she made sure my expectations to compete athletically extended to expectations to excel academically. My high school teachers—Coach Zavada, Mr. Schaad, Mr. Delger, Mr. Sommerville, Ms. Krejerek, Mrs. Hucke, Ms. Good, Mrs. Romanoski, and Mrs. Bluel—all helped me stay focused on what I wanted to do in the future, which was go to college. Mrs. Klescewski (Mrs. K) helped me daily as my classroom aide, assisting with homework and making sure I was prepared and organized. She made sure I was always pushed toward my full potential.

It wasn't until later that I recognized what Mrs. Schmid, Mrs. K, and all the other teachers and aides did for me with their expectations of me. To them, I was just AJ, and other than getting around in an awesome chair, there was nothing different about me. They allowed me to be myself. They allowed me to believe I could do anything. They always kept the focus on what could be done. What I didn't realize until later was how well every person involved in my life found a way to help put me in a position to be successful. The start they gave me would continue through college and continues today into my next phase in life.

Then there is my extended family . . .

The Maki Family

Mrs. Maki: When I was very young, Mrs. Maki made me a hat that looked like a bomber plane and side banners for my power wheelchair. I ran all around the track during football games celebrating being a bomber.

Ty: It was Ty who came over when the girls were babysitting. He would kneel down and stand me up so I could play tackle football with Douglas. On Saturdays, he would take me to the T-ball program, stand me up, and help me swing the bat. After a hit, he would pick me up, tuck me under his arm, and we would run around the bases together. Sometimes I didn't think he was giving it his all, and I would ask him, "Can't you go any faster?"

Casey: Casey was my favorite basketball player when I was growing up. He always made me feel part of the team even though I was only seven years old. When Kohler won state basketball in 1999, he came out of the locker room and went right to me and said, "We did it!" and gave me a high five.

Alise: Alise traveled with us everywhere. We took her to California to watch the Packers play. That was the first time she had ever flown in an airplane. We took her to Chicago, too. My parents said we always had to have the same number of adults as kids.

Mr. Maki: Mr. Maki was my go-to guy for all the boys' and girls' basketball games. My parents would put me on his lap as we watched the games. Mr. Maki would call the officials nicknames based on whom he thought they looked like. Between Mr. Maki and Mr. Zimmermann, I would almost soil myself laughing. My family always said that Mr. Maki and Mr. Zimmermann reminded them of the Muppets in the balcony, Statler and Waldorf. They always had something to say.

Joe Balge: Joe took me to Camp Y Coda, the YMCA day camp. With his help, I did everything including shooting a bow and arrow and going down the giant water slide. What a great time.

Basketball Players/Babysitters

Suzanna Wood and Dawn Taubenheim were not only on my dad's first basketball team, they were also our first babysitters. They would come over and kick out my mom and dad. I guess they thought my parents needed some time without the kids. They would then play with us. It was a win for all of us. Their fee for babysitting was a 12-pack of Mountain Dew and a bag of Doritos. Sometimes they would bring Katie McClary with them. She was always someone I could talk to about the game.

After Suzanna, Dawn, and Katie graduated, Corey Biersdorf, Pam Free, and Emily Grube were next in line. They were all great.

In that same class was Katie Dickelman. Even though she was young, she probably had the most impact on me, and I believe I had a great impact on her and who she is today. Early on, Katie would come to my therapy sessions. She was with us in Minnesota when the doctor told me I would never walk. I think she was as disappointed that day as the rest of my family was. I truly believe I helped inspire her to get her doctorate in physical therapy. I know she always made me feel like I could do anything as I grew up.

The final group of babysitters were Nicole Campbell, Megan McClary, and Annie Salzwedal. They always came as a twosome or threesome. Just like Dawn and Suzanna had done years prior, Nicole, Megan, and Annie would chase my parents out of the house while they hung out with my brothers and me.

Before I leave the babysitters, I need to give a special thank you to one family who watched over me as I grew up and honored me in a very special way when I graduated from high school—the McClary family (Mr. John, Mrs. Patti, Katie, Megan, and Erin). It was at Honors Night during senior year when I was called to the stage to receive the McClary family scholarship. As I mentioned above, Katie and Megan both played basketball for my dad. Dad also practiced basketball a great deal with the youngest McClary, Erin. This award was very special for many reasons. The McClary family was a great supporter of Kohler school both academically and athletically, especially basketball. More importantly, Mrs. McClary and Katie weren't able to be on stage presenting me that evening. Mrs. McClary had passed away of cancer the previous year. Katie, who my dad always said was the most passionate player he ever coached, died tragically her sophomore year at Duke University. I believe Mrs. McClary and Katie were there that night, just not on stage.

It was great growing up with all the players/babysitters. They were the best. Thank you, Dad, for coaching and opening the door to so many friends.

All of these people and so many more have come into my life and made a difference. I can't thank all of you enough for everything you have done for me.

Finally, My Family

They have been there since I was 3 lbs. 14oz. You have heard about the parents and my two brothers. You have heard about how I got my name from my two grandpas.

Then there were my grandmas. Grandma Kay loved to bake and spoiled me every time I went to visit her at the lake. Grandma Char was my number one fan, as she went to all of my events, no matter the weather.

My aunts (Boo, Di, Jeannie, Daryl, Cindy, Donna, Amy), uncles (Randy, Jim, Dave, Mark, Bob, Monte), cousins (Rachelle, Matt, Jon, Jamie, Andrew, Kristin, Marla, Mike, Justin, Nicholas).

This group believed in me and never let me stop believing in myself. They helped me become who I am today. They considered "I can't" a swear word. All of them together gave me an opportunity to FINISH.

Thank you.

"The best NCAA tournament game this weekend wasn't on your bracket."

The following article was written March 24, 2014, for *USA Today*, following UW–Whitewater's men's basketball team's second national championship in three years.

"He's been an absolute inspiration to our team."

After the confetti stopped raining down and the Warhawks accepted their trophy, the players and staff surrounded the basket in front of their bench and started individually climbing the ladder to each cut down a piece of the net. The first strand didn't go to a player or even to someone with the ability to cut it down on his own.

That fabric instead went to 22-year-old AJ Bocchini, a team manager for the past three seasons who has become an integral part of the group. Bocchini, who is confined to a wheelchair due to cerebral palsy, will graduate next year and hopes of coaching at the Division III level at some point in the future.

Bocchini's father, a high school athletic director, asked Miller when Bocchini enrolled if there was any way to get him involved with the team. He ended up handling the team's shot clock during home games and becoming one of the locker room's most spirited personalities in the process.

"I don't know if I've ever been around anyone as passionate about basketball, particularly Warhawk basketball, as AJ," Miller said. "We got him in the huddle on Thursday at practice and his message to the guys was 'FINISH.' He's gone from being a guy who kind of hung around to a leader. He's a leader of this team, and he inspires guys. You look at the adversity he faces and what he's willing to go through to be with us, travel with us, be part of our program. You can't help but look at the guy and love the kid."

2012 National Champions

Wearing the 2012 National Championship net

Celebrating with Cody - 2012 National Champions

2014 National Champions

Selfie with Calvin after 2014 Championship

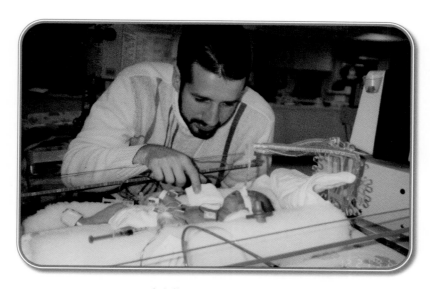

Dad chilling at St Mary's hospital

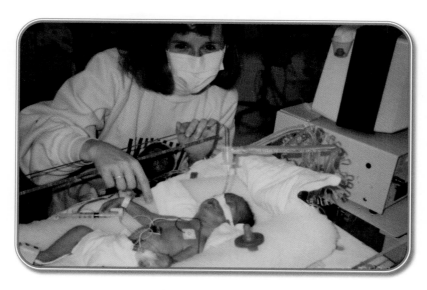

Mom hanging out in the hospital

Snuggling with Grandma Char

Namesakes - Grandpa Joe and Grandpa Tony

Going for a ride with Mom and Douglas

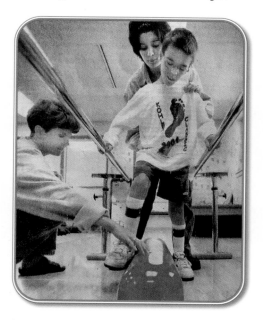

Brenda and Mom walking with AJ through the parallel bars

Getting ready to play flag football
with Mr. Maki

Bocchini boys with best friend Ace

Ty Maki playing T-ball with AJ "Ty, can't you run any faster?"

Alise Maki, AJ and
Dominic in California

Coach/teacher Mr. DuMez

Playing soccer with Mom

Coach Buhr's halftime speech

Middle School Track meet. AJ lane 4, Douglas lane 1

Riding with teammates in the homecoming parade

Head Football coach Matt Zavada

Athletic Director/Football Coach Al Holzheimer

Grandma Kay at AJ's game

Douglas and AJ after the big win over Sheboygan Falls

AJ and cousin Michael leading the team out for Senior night

Rudy Award - Thank you Kohler and Lutheran Schools

Post Season Basketball Banquet Senior year with Kohler coaches -
Larry Kampman (Kampy), Ken Roeder, Kyle Gebler

Mr. McClary and Megan presenting AJ with the McClary Foundation Scholarship

High school graduation with the family

Therapist team - Jodi Wagner, Brenda Schilder, Carol Harpold, Kelly Dirkse, Gail Slaughter at AJ's High school graduation party

Assistant Coach Mike Rittgers (St Catherines)

Having lunch with Mrs. D.

Mike Lenzer
(UW–Whitewater) Physical Therapy

Out to lunch in Racine with Kaitlin and Dylan

Principal Hansen during speech at
Howards Grove Middle School

AD John Johnson and Assistant
Coach Mike Rittgers at St. Catherines

Family visiting friends John and Martha Schott

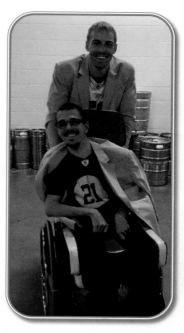

Packer game day Embassadors -
Eric Bryson and AJ

Cody, AJ and Eric at Dylan and Kaitlin's wedding

Dad, Kaitlin, AJ, Philly, Mom and Dylan out on the town

UW–Whitewater graduation

Showing off the bling - 2012 National Championship ring